PORTFOLIO C

METROPOLITAN SEMINARS IN ART

Great Periods in Painting

PORTFOLIO C

The World Rediscovered: THE EARLY RENAISSANCE

BY JOHN CANADAY

ART EDITOR AND CRITIC
THE NEW YORK TIMES

THE METROPOLITAN MUSEUM OF ART

THE WORLD REDISCOVERED

The Early Renaissance

THE Renaissance was not so much a rebirth as a change in the direction of thought. Man began to see himself as an individual who controlled his own destiny, rather than a soul who must serve a dangerous earthly testing period to determine whether he would spend eternity in bliss or damnation. The world ceased to be a divine miracle to be accepted on faith and explained by theology and became, instead, a natural phenomenon to be explained on its own terms.

The ancient Greeks and Romans had also accepted the world as a fact to be understood and a place to be enjoyed. To this extent the Renaissance was indeed a rebirth, the rebirth of a way of thought leading to the revival of the arts and ideas of classical antiquity. But in the meantime the mystical experience of the Middle Ages had become ineradicably a part of Western philosophy. The special character of the Renaissance was that it fused Christian and pagan elements in its nature, adding to them the objective curiosity that was the genesis of modern scientific investigation.

Like the Greeks the men of the Renaissance wanted to know everything, to understand everything; like the Romans they loved display, power, and luxury; as Christians, they drew upon the emotionalism that had revealed new depths in the mystery of darkness and new intensities in the radiance of light.

The pictures we are about to examine are expressions of renaissance thought painted during the same years as the medieval art we have just discussed. This chronological contradiction is confusing, but all we need remember is that we are tracing the rise of one age that coincided with the decline of another, that an age of passionate curiosity was flowering in Italy as the age of faith was on the wane in the north.

Saint Francis of Assisi

Saint Francis of Assisi (1182–1226) lived two hundred years before 1400, the arbitrary date at which we open the Renaissance in Italy. He is often called the climactic figure of the Middle Ages and, just as often, the prophet of the Renaissance—for he was both. Although he was born into a century that regarded life as something to be avoided, a degradation and a prison, he revealed the world to be a joyous place. The fundamental principle of his philosophy was joy—delight in life, even in amusement. To the Franciscans, the order of friars he founded, life was an adventure, a balance of ugliness and beauty, evil and good. Saint Francis aroused his century to this attitude; his Hymn of the Sun (*Cantico del sole*) is almost pagan in its worship of nature, recalling the lyric pastoral poetry of ancient Rome, with the difference, of course, that for Saint Francis all nature is a manifestation of God.

The Franciscan order spread tremendously, even into the guilds and the higher classes of society. The Franciscans were divided into three orders, the first composed of men vowed to poverty, obedience, and chastity; the second

5

Figure 1

a women's order along the same lines, under Saint Clare; the third a group of men and women living in the world, married and raising families if they wished, but pledged to Franciscan principles as applied to their busy lives. Members were supposed to contribute not only their wealth but their efforts and talents.

Thousands of people were members of this third order; the movement was so widespread that it could not but find its expression in art. An early reflection is the fresco cycle, completed just before 1300, in the saint's church at Assisi. One episode, *Saint Francis Preaching to the Birds* (Plate C1), is one of the best-loved pictures in the history of art, and with reason.

In the first place, it tells a delightful story: the saint is shown fulfilling his promise to a flock of birds to preach a sermon especially for them if they remained quiet while he finished talking to his human followers. The attentive little creatures, about to be joined by a late-comer hurrying down from the branches of a tree, are receiving the full attention of the gentle saint. He is obviously making a serious point in clear, simple terms, bending forward a little toward his feathered parishioners and gesturing with both hands.

But the story only partially accounts for the delightfulness of the painting. The anecdote is just as clearly told by Bonaventura Berlinghieri, a painter associated with the early Franciscan movement, in his large panel, *Saint Francis and Scenes from His Life* (*Figure 1*). Berlinghieri has his own importance as a painter who warmed and freshened the Byzantine tradition by using its conventions with inventive informality. His *Saint Francis* is a beautiful panel, with its gold, its bright color, and its enchanting patterns. In the episode showing Saint Francis preaching to the birds (*Figure 2*), the stylized rock forms, the plants that grow from them, looking like designs for brooches (with blossoms for jewels), the vivacious silhouettes of the birds, the stiff figures of the saint and his companions, the diminutive stage-scenery church behind them tell

aptly and clearly enough what is going on.

But these forms, with the possible exception of the birds, are conventionalized to the point of becoming symbols; the Assisi fresco (Plate C1) gives us, instead, forms we can believe in as real. In other words, the painter of the fresco has humanized the subject, painting it as if he were re-creating a scene he had actually witnessed. By comparison, the earlier panel is a richly ornamented diagram.

To reproduce real forms, the forms of the world Saint Francis loved, the fresco painter abandoned the conventional representation of drapery, hands, and heads in patterned lines for realistic masses revealed by light and shade.

Figure 2

The arms of the saint may be too long and his body may be ambiguous under the robes, but *Saint Francis Preaching to the Birds*, seen against the background of painting until that time, represents a tremendous revolution in the way the world was seen and recorded.

Giotto

Until recently the Assisi frescoes were attributed to Giotto di Bondone (1266 or 1276–1337), and it was pleasant to believe that

7

Giotto, a member of the third Franciscan order, painted them as his contribution to the organization. Contemporary scholars hesitate to accept the attribution, but the frescoes, whether by Giotto or by someone closely related to him, have a revolutionary degree of realism. They bring us close to the spirit of Saint Francis because the world is painted as a tangible fact.

Technical discoveries, in this case the techniques of realism, are unimportant except as means to an end. Giotto's end was the exploration of psychological values that demanded realistic forms for expression. In his great work, the fresco cycle in the Arena Chapel in Padua, this end is powerfully attained. The Arena cycle was painted about 1305, only a few years after the Assisi frescoes. If Giotto painted the earlier cycle, he developed tremendously during those years, from sweet and gentle storytelling to dramatic grandeur.

The technical advance is great also; the occasionally tentative forms in the Assisi frescoes are replaced by consistently full and assured

Figure 3

forms, corresponding to the deepening and widening psychological revelation. We have already seen the Arena Chapel (Portfolio 8, *Figure 7*) and two of the frescoes, the supreme *Lamentation over the Body of Christ* (Portfolio 8, *Figure 8* and Plate 89) and *Joachim's Dream* (Portfolio 8, *Figure 9* and Plate 90). Two more examples will remind us of Giotto's range: the deeply tender emotion of *The Visitation* (*Figure 3*) and the dramatic psychological interplay between Christ and Judas in *The Betrayal* (detail, *Figure 4*).

The Visitation is played against a Giotto background of dollhouselike architecture, for in spite of the solidity of his major forms Giotto was unable to cope with the problem of fully integrated space and full-scale architecture in perspective. But in terms of sentiment he leaves us in no doubt about the nature of the greeting exchanged by Elisabeth and the Virgin Mary.

The Betrayal is psychologically more complex but equally successful. Christ's head is nobly erect; the head of Judas is half buried in the folds of his robe, like a predatory animal about to spring or a serpent ready to strike. His face reveals with absolute clarity a complex state of mind: lips pursed, Judas meets the eyes of Christ and realizes that the false kiss is recognized for what it is. The betrayer's fear pulls for a moment against his greed; shame and regret, just beneath the surface, are overwhelmed by the compulsive forward movement of the act, which, we know, will be completed after this dividing instant of hesitation.

Although the subject is part of a religious story, it is conceived as a drama of human motivation in which Christ and Judas are individuals, unique psychological entities, rather than characters enacting standard roles. Giotto's art, like the philosophy of Saint Francis, may be regarded as a medieval summation, but Giotto, even more than Saint Francis, shows us the way to the Renaissance. The medieval religious fervor of the Arena frescoes is undeniable, but sections like *The Betrayal* are

Figure 4

renaissance in their emphasis on the individual and their exploration of the nature of man.

When Giotto painted the Arena frescoes nearly seven hundred years ago he set the direction that Western art has followed ever since. Not until we come to the twentieth century and modern abstract art, which denies the association between expression and representation, is Giotto's basic premise rejected.

Masaccio and Florence

Giotto's contribution was not enlarged by his contemporaries nor by his followers for three generations afterward. For a hundred years he remained the model for Italian painters. Even in Siena, a conservative stronghold of medieval style, the brothers Pietro and Ambrogio Lorenzetti introduced Giotto's naturalism into Sienese painting (*Figure 5*) and might have transformed it if they had not died in the plague of 1348. As it was, none of the Giotteschi ("Giotto-like" painters) who worked elsewhere reached Giotto's stature. They polished his forms, elaborated them, and even made advances in perspective, of which Giotto was innocent, and in accurate representation of the proportions of the body. But these were surface advances. The Giottesque painters never approached their master in emotional

9

power and human insight, and at the end of the fourteenth century Italian painting was still Gothic in feeling and style.

But the opening of the fifteenth century coincided with the birth of a painter of incredible genius. Masaccio died before he was thirty, but in his few years he took up the art of painting where Giotto had left it (as is always said) and carried it to the point we might have expected it to reach if three generations of Giottesque painters had produced great talents instead of secondary ones.

Masaccio collaborated on occasion with an older painter, Masolino da Panicale (1383– about 1447), a Florentine much affected by the international style. He has been called Masaccio's teacher, but in effect Masaccio was not taught by anyone. He seems to have painted with inborn knowledge of how to represent in deep space nobly proportioned forms logically revealed by light and shade—in short, he seems to have inherited Giotto's intention and to have fulfilled it through a phenomenal natural ability, free from the last of Giotto's technical limitations. We know no more of his method of study—we can only assume that it was systematic, even scientific—than the artists who tried to discover it after Masaccio's death, when his frescoes replaced Giotto's as the source to which painters came to learn.

With Masaccio every awkwardness and inaccuracy of proportion vanish; Giotto's toy architecture, so out of keeping with his stately figures, becomes in paintings like *The Holy Trinity* (*Figure 6*) a fully realized and harmonious formal structure defining spatial volumes. And Masaccio is a worthy follower of Giotto in dramatic expression. The agony of shame in *The Expulsion of Adam and Eve from Paradise* (*Figure 7*) is expressed as Giotto would have expressed it, by faces that reflect inner feeling and by bodily attitudes that would tell the story alone if the faces were obliterated or, like Adam's here, hidden. Masaccio's forms always have reference to the appearance of a world of flesh and blood and volume, rather

than to a formula of line and symbol. Giotto and he are inevitably identified with one another: Giotto innovated and Masaccio fulfilled a single conception of the art of painting.

Masaccio, with Donatello the sculptor and Brunelleschi the architect (who may have designed the renaissance architecture painted by Masaccio in *The Holy Trinity*), introduced the unprecedented burst of creation that took place in Florence during the next decades and ushered in the Renaissance. In this small city every other man seemed to have been born to carve, to build, and especially to paint. The artists were skilled craftsmen and creative spirits of the greatest inventiveness, originality, and perception; their patrons were enlightened

Figure 5

10

men who vied with one another for their services. In the workshops of a dozen masters, a dozen individual styles bore witness to the independence, the restlessness, the explorative vigor of the Florentine temperament; wealthy families competed in building churches and palaces and commissioning their ornamentation until they created a city that, today, is one great museum.

Discarding Gothic forms in architecture, the Florentines studied their classical heritage and adapted it to their own uses. (*The Holy Trinity* shows a return to the round, coffered vault of Rome and to the conception of architecture as an exercise in clarity and proportion instead of a mystical flight toward heaven.) Painters and sculptors dissected bodies to understand better how to draw them; they worked as mathematicians to codify the laws of perspective; they read the legends and philosophies of antiquity, led there by their rediscovery of the world as a wonderful place belonging to them.

The Gothic spirit, where it survived, borrowed forms from this new world. Fra Angelico (1387–1455), a member of the Dominican order, never hesitated to adopt the discoveries of his more worldly and more adventurous contemporaries. His *Annunciation* (*Figure 8*) is staged in a renaissance setting, a Florentine loggia copied from the architect Michelozzo, but he represents the event with placid and unquestioning acceptance of its actuality. This acceptance characterizes his art and gives it conviction in an age that was learning to question all values. Fra Angelico's is the last sweet and pure medieval voice in Italy, rising clear and true among the more vigorous ones of his Florentine compatriots.

Pageantry and Perspective

One of these compatriots, Fra Filippo Lippi (about 1406–1469), was quick to adopt the appealing sweetness of Fra Angelico, modifying it toward a worldliness more in keeping with his time and certainly more in keeping with his

Figure 6

character, as will soon become quite apparent.

The Madonna in Fra Filippo's *Virgin Adoring the Child* (*Figure 9*) is a descendant of Fra Angelico's, if you wish, but her piety is a bit deceptive. She is so irresistibly attractive that we can forget that what we really have here is only a pretty girl, her healthy child, ragamuffins pressed into the job of posing as angels, and a happy decorative landscape. We also forget that, unlike Fra Angelico, this painter-monk was a man of the world, constantly in and out of court, sued for this and that, and convicted of forgery on one occasion. His most spectacular defection was the seduction of a young nun (he was chaplain of her convent) named Lucrezia Buti, who was to bear him two children, one of whom became the painter Filippino Lippi. These transgressions were glossed over in a Florence that could forgive a great deal when the sinner was an artist of talent. Fra Filippo fared very well.

11

Figure 7

Among his more pretentious works, *The Funeral of Saint Stephen* (*Figure 10*) shows how efficiently and uninterestingly Fra Filippo could paint a group of rather bored men attending a supposedly imposing occasion. He draws from Masaccio's *Tribute Money* (Portfolio 8, Plate 86) for their arrangement and

from his *Holy Trinity* for the deep perspective background, but he makes no effort to continue Masaccio's exalted human drama. He picks up pointers on how Masaccio achieved his illusion of solid forms in space and applies them to his lesser ends. But the mundane spirit of *The Funeral of Saint Stephen* and the charming, essentially worldly sweetness of *The Virgin Adoring the Child* set a pattern that was followed by large numbers of painters.

It would be wearisome, of course, if every painter were as monumental as Masaccio. We also need smaller men, like another of Masaccio's contemporaries, Paolo Uccello (about 1396–1475). He was equally interested in the creation of space by means of perspective, but whereas Masaccio uses space as the setting for profound drama and Lippi as a background for rather stuffy formal ceremonies, Uccello's space is a combination of enthusiastic scientific demonstration and decorative invention.

Uccello was an early investigator of perspective. The most familiar story about him is that he was so obsessed with the subject that he cried out in his sleep, declaring his love for "thou delightful perspective"; his wife thereupon accused him of infidelity with a lady named "Prospectiva." This story is somehow in keeping with the fancifulness and the half-naive quality of most of Uccello's works, including a series of battle scenes painted before 1457 for the palace of the Medici to commemorate a Florentine victory over Milan at San Romano.

The panels are now dispersed in three museums—the Louvre in Paris, the Uffizi in Florence, and the National Gallery in London. The London panel, *The Rout of San Romano* (Plate C2), is especially rich in the tapestrylike effect created by the turbaned and armored warriors mounted on handsomely arrayed horses. It is especially entertaining—the word is not meant to be condescending—in its demonstration of perspective. The fallen knight at lower left, the broken lances, and other battle gear lying on the ground have been carefully disposed in parallel lines receding from the observer. This arrangement has little to do with the confusion of battle, but it does give Uccello an opportunity to diagram the perspective principle of parallel lines converging toward a common vanishing point.

It is usually said that the crisscrossed lances of the warriors, the many breaks and interruptions of forms, and the strong contrasts of color express the confusion of battle. But this forces the point. The end effect of *The Rout of San Romano* is that of a well-staged pageant, fashionable and exciting, rather than a bloody and desperate battle.

The Florentines were fond of pageantry and masters of it. The Medici, like other leading Florentine families, organized spectacular public processions and ceremonies for all sorts of important occasions, including weddings and the coming of age of sons, somewhat in the tradition of the spectacles offered to the public by Roman emperors to take people's minds off unpleasant things like increased taxes. Leading artists designed the temporary architecture, including triumphal arches (another Roman echo), costumes, and paraphernalia. There was nothing slipshod or offhand about these pageants, and their preparation included the commissioning of important works of art as mementos of the event.

The Youthful David (Plate C3) by Andrea del Castagno (1423–1457) is a parade shield, which explains its unusual shape; it is also one of the finest paintings by an important artist with few known works.

Castagno was one of the most forceful of the Florentine painters, which means that his hard-bitten realism was forceful indeed. His forms are as sculpturesque as they are painterly, as scientific and analytical as those of the sculptor Donatello, whose investigations of the techniques of realism inspired painters as much as Masaccio's. Castagno was one of the fervent anatomists of the early Renaissance, but *The Youthful David* is no mere exercise in anatomical truth. The almost harsh vitality of the young body would be fascinating but meaningless if it did not serve also as a reflection of intangibles. The youth is more than an iron-muscled athlete who has killed a giant; he is the triumph of good over the monstrous forces of evil, represented by the head of Goliath, with David's stone embedded in its forehead, lying at his feet.

The Youthful David is one of those wonderful paintings in which every element serves several functions simultaneously. As pure design it is impeccable. The hard but sinuous lines of the fluttering outer garment contrast with the angularities of the rock ledges; the arclike lines of the foliage spring upward in counterforce to the curvature of the shield, leading us back to the center of the picture as the sides of the shield turn away from it. The serpentine locks of hair and small, intense clouds, played against the flat, dark blue sky; the upward-converging lines of the figure, countered by the reversed slant of the sides of the shield; the forward rush of the body, brought into balance by the turning of the head in the opposite direction and the upraised arm—everywhere we are held within a system of tensions and counter-tensions, rhythms and counter-rhythms, of powerful abstract beauty and great expressive force. David rises gigantically against the sky, a colossus above the landscape, dwarfing the river that curves behind him. The youth who killed the giant has become a giant, declaring thus emphatically the triumph of good.

In a medieval painting we would more probably have had a delicate stripling who killed his enemy with the aid of a miracle through faith. But *The Youthful David* was painted by a renaissance man who believed that good must triumph through the intellectual force of individual responsibility. There is nothing Greek about the forms Castagno has painted, but there is a parallel to the Greek idea that the body may be painted or carved as an image of inner nature. The forms differ because the Greek ideal was one of perfect intellectual and physical harmony, whereas Castagno's ideal is one of moral force. Castagno has abandoned medieval faith in miracle but not the Christian concern with the war between good and evil.

Pageantry and Daily Life

These ideological considerations have taken us a great distance from parade shields and renaissance pageantry. We are in danger of no such digression in discussing the art of Domenico Ghirlandaio (1449–1494). We are back in the daily world of Florence, where, on the evidence of Ghirlandaio's painting, domestic pageantry provided almost as rich a spectacle as public celebrations.

Ghirlandaio spent his life painting frescoes of biblical stories conceived as polite social events in which leading citizens participated, thus continuing, in a second generation, the tradition of Fra Filippo Lippi. In Ghirlandaio's *Birth of the Virgin* (*Figure 11*), for instance, it takes us a moment to find the new-born child. One sees first, as was intended, a Florentine lady, with an entourage of attendant friends, who has called to offer her congratulations to Saint Anne. The visitor is probably Lodovica Tornabuoni, a member of one of the wealthy families that commissioned many pictures like this one from Ghirlandaio; he returned the compliment by casting them in conspicuous roles, even when his dramas, as in the case of *The Birth of the Virgin*, were painted on the walls of churches.

Painters like Ghirlandaio, who lack imagination, are often at their best in the fashionable portrait, which demands purely objective representation, modified by a little tactful beautifying. Portraiture flourished in Florence, a city where individualism was the rule of life

Alinari

Figure 8

Figure 9

and self-display a rule of social conduct. Technical execution and sheer objective brilliance sometimes raised Ghirlandaio's portraits to the level of creative art, as in *A Lady of the Sassetti Family* (Plate C4). This portrait tells us nothing of the sitter's character except whatever we deduce, with no assurance of being right, from her precisely represented exterior, including coiffure, jewels, and dress, which are given as much prominence as the face. But the consistent objectivity with which detail is selected and manipulated to produce an image of exceptional unity evokes one surface of an age that put its faith in tangible things and investigated them unflinchingly. By this standard the art of Ghirlandaio becomes more than a factual record of the world in which his patrons lived and moved. It becomes a declaration of principle—the principle that we can discover the meaning of the world only by beginning with its objective facts.

Space, Architecture, and Men

The ornamented column, the capital, the frieze of cupids, and the wall panels of the Florentine palace where Ghirlandaio staged his *Birth of the Virgin* show how completely renaissance architects had abandoned medieval forms and how freely they adapted classical ones. The forms and methods of medieval architecture discussed in the preceding portfolio had never been more than halfheartedly used in Italy. Italian builders were less daring in their use of the vault, employed the flying buttress hardly at all, and generally continued the simpler pattern of the very early Christian churches. When we come to the Renaissance, the architects seem to turn with relief and excitement to the revival of classical forms, with their round arches and vaults, their more arbitrarily calculated proportions, and their human rather than spiritual character.

The early renaissance architect was more designer than engineer. Visitors to Italy are often disturbed by the many disfiguring tie rods, iron braces introduced across arches to keep them from spreading and falling. The architect designed the arches for beauty of proportion, without determining whether they were capable of standing without help. The subterfuge of the tie rod would have been unthinkable to a cathedral architect in France, where design and engineering were all but synonymous. This identity between the esthetic and the structural aspects of a building is the essence of the modern "functional" idea; hence modern architects are likely to admire French Gothic but to reject early renaissance, accusing the designers of being essentially painters rather than builders and referring to them as "paper architects."

There is some justice in this accusation. Painting was certainly more sympathetic to the renaissance spirit. It was the most flexible art, allowing the widest variety of individual expression and most directly adaptable to the restlessness and enthusiasm of the early renais-

Figure 10

sance intellect, which explored in all directions. For this reason some of the period's most beautiful buildings were never constructed and were never intended to be; they are the painted architecture in pictures like *The Birth of the Virgin* (Plate C5), attributed to Fra Carnevale (active 1456–died 1484), who was also an architect and engineer for the dukes of Urbino.

Here is a wonderfully lucid and pearly building, open to the warm Italian air, with exquisitely tooled and proportioned moldings, capitals, bas-reliefs, ornamental swags, and medallions derived from ancient Rome. The pictured events are not much less social in character than Ghirlandaio's, but there is a difference: here the figures move with grave and stately elegance in architectural space. They are richly costumed, but their sobriety is respectful to the occasion and to the dignity of the monument that Fra Carnevale designed as a setting worthy of the event.

As in Ghirlandaio's version, the most conspicuous figures are the relatively incidental people in the foreground, who assume beautifully quiet attitudes, trailing their capes and robes upon the marble terrace. But they are appropriately separated from the holy event by a shallow flight of steps running across the

composition from border to border, creating a low stage where the bathing of the child takes place. By contrast, Ghirlandaio's gossipy interior falls just short of vulgarity.

It is possible to compare Ghirlandaio to a society photographer and his *Birth of the Virgin* to one of those pictures in the Sunday paper showing socially prominent ladies opening a charity bazaar, but no such comparison holds for the scene as represented by Fra Carnevale. Neither painting has emotional depth of religious conviction, but Ghirlandaio's scene is mundane in an obvious way, whereas Fra Carnevale's picture, with its logical disposition of quiet forms in deep space, suggests a new ideal, a civilization where elegance need not be confused with vanity, where order may be produced by intellectual discipline without sacrificing the delights offered by the world of the senses.

The importance attached to perspective in renaissance painting is explained by the desire to create space in which such a world could appropriately exist, worldly space rather than celestial, space that could be ordered harmoniously and rationally as a fitting habitation for renaissance man. The materialism of renaissance life created a new ideal: the com-

16

plete man, the individual who could master all experience and learning and finally leave the world knowing that he had made the most of his time as part of it.

This was a goal beyond the conception or the hope of most men, but among intellectuals of the Renaissance who were born to wealth and position it came as close to realization as it was ever to do in any age. In Florence there was Lorenzo de' Medici, always called "the Magnificent," a shrewd politician, a dangerous enemy, a poet, a philosopher, and, where he failed of self-fulfillment, the munificent patron who enabled other men to enrich the world of art and science. At the court of Urbino, where Fra Carnevale worked, there was Federigo da Montefeltro (1422–1482), a soldier and statesman and the most learned member of his learned court—a philosopher, theologian, scientist, historian, and of course, a connoisseur of the arts.

A small study (*Figure 12*) created for Federigo in his residence at Gubbio is, at first glance, a fantastic novelty and, upon consideration, a tribute to Federigo's learning and a statement of the identity of art and science in the Renaissance. The room is a masterpiece of *trompe l'oeil*, "fool-the-eye" perspective, executed entirely in wood inlay. The doors to wall cupboards seem to stand open; shelves appear to hold objects in the apparent spaces back of the open doors; pilasters with capitals seem to occupy the angles of walls; benches seem to project into the room, even to cast shadows. But all these things—doors, shelves, closets, pilasters and capitals, benches, even shadows —are "painted" in different woods, cut to size and pieced together in a perfectly flat surface.

By any standard this is an amazing piece of work, something to startle anybody, something to fascinate, endlessly, a child. Beyond that, the scheme is a tribute to the "complete man," in the person of the duke. The open doors of the illusionistic cupboards reveal a cittern, a pair of dividers, and an hour glass; there are other symbols of art, science, and

Alinari

Figure 11

Figure 12

learning in the form of books, arms (the duke was a master of the art of war), writing materials, quadrants, a celestial globe, and even such minor items as a box of sweets and a birdcage with a parakeet.

But the final significance, the real meaning of the study, lies beyond optical tricks and even beyond the tribute to the duke's learning. It tells us that the renaissance artist's deification of perspective, by which he created and organized the objects of this world in three-dimensional space, reflected the determination of renaissance man to fulfill himself by controlling nature through knowledge of its laws. For the artist the first of these laws was optical perspective, which enabled him to organize a world of logical and convincing reality.

The science of perspective was finally summarized by the painter Piero della Francesca, who compiled his treatises between about 1478, when he gave up painting for pure mathematics, and his death in 1492. Masaccio, through the Brancacci Chapel frescoes, and Donatello, Brunelleschi, and another architect, Alberti, through personal acquaintance, contributed to Piero's triumph, by which the visible world was disciplined by mathematical order. But in his own painting before that time Piero had consummated the renaissance marriage of art and science in his representation of space in the Arezzo frescoes (Portfolio 4, *Figure 16*, and Portfolio 8, *Figure 5* and Plate 85). He painted *The Madonna and Child with Saints and Angels* (Portfolio 6, Plate 67), which we have analyzed as a spatial composition, for Federigo da Montefeltro, who appears in it, at the lower right, in adoration.

Another portrait of the duke, *Federigo da*

Montefeltro, Duke of Urbino (Plate C6), also by Piero, is one of the extraordinary portraits of any time, a supreme example of the revelation of personality in spite of seemingly insuperable difficulties. A jousting accident had cost the duke his right eye and had broken the nose in a face already swarthy and far from ideally beautiful. But Piero took the ruined profile, the coarse hair, even the warts on the face, and patterned them into a design revealing the strength, decision, intelligence, and abstract beauty—for, as drawn by Piero, the line of the duke's profile has become abstractly beautiful—of one of the most compelling personalities of the age.

The portrait is paired, framed as a diptych, with one of Federigo's wife, Battista Sforza (*Figure 13*). Battista, alongside Federigo's dark skin, black hair, and singing red robe, is pale, almost characterless, bearing the weight of her jewels and ornamental ribbons with more patience than style. There are various explanations for the drop in power between the portraits. A likely one is that Battista, who was only twenty when the picture was painted, simply did not offer the material for a portrait of equal psychological depth.

Umbrian Painting

With Piero della Francesca and Fra Carnevale we have left Florence for Umbria. With them, and with Ghirlandaio, we have left the first half of the fifteenth century, with development centered in Florence, and have entered the period when Florentine ideas were absorbed and enlarged in Italy as a whole. Each major city-state of the peninsula reflected special characteristics in its art; each modified local traditions from the medieval past and created new ones in the spirit of the new age.

The region of Umbria offers the most dulcet vistas in Italy, deep, clear blue distances, gentle mountains, and sweet valleys; not surprisingly, therefore, landscape took on a special importance in Umbrian painting. Florentine artists approached landscape as a record of topography; in Umbria, it became poetry. The landscape backgrounds in Piero's portrait of Federigo and his wife and in the allegories on the reverse (*Figure 14*) are dominated by the foreground figures and marred by the fact that, although they are conceived as a single stretch of land, they are interrupted in the middle. Still, these backgrounds offer a lyrical world of fields and rivers spotted with small trees, boats, and castles, stretching along bits of road through hills until eventually they disappear into the light. As accessories to the portraits, these deep landscapes bestow a greater prominence on the heads, isolating them in space and giving them eminence and grandeur by the sudden contrast in scale. Imagine the head of the duke with a piece of tapestry as a background and this function of the landscape becomes apparent.

A landscape can enhance the mood of a picture; the role of the serene background behind Federigo becomes clear if we imagine his profile played against a stormy scene: our previous impression of the great clarity and decision of his intellect would be much changed. Piero uses landscape as an adjunct to mood even more conspicuously in *The Resurrection* (Portfolio 8, Plate 91), where Christ, placed between bare trees on one side and leafy saplings on the other, rises against a sky lightening with dawn.

The general character of Umbrian painting is sweet, sometimes oversweet, but obviously this criticism cannot be made of Piero's art. He was as much a Florentine as an Umbrian, as was Luca Signorelli (about 1441–1523), one of several painters given credit for being the first to study anatomy through dissection. Signorelli found his perfect subject matter in a series of frescoes illustrating the Last Judgment; he could show masses of naked figures straining and writhing in every attitude of hope, anguish, and despair (*Figure 15*). But the typical Umbrian painter was not much interested in experiments or in the scientific investigation of space and anatomy. He was content to follow, as a provincial, the discoveries made elsewhere. The leader of the school, Pietro Perugino (1445–1523), was a skillful workman who found a good formula and stuck to it. At his best he painted irreproachably, if we forgive him a certain obviousness and lack of power; his landscape backgrounds are minor pastoral lyrics (Portfolio 6, Plate 64). But his sweetness eventually becomes cloying, like a meal made up of a series of desserts.

Perugino was tremendously successful; he had more orders than he could fill, even though he used stock patterns that he varied slightly from picture to picture. He gathered about himself a small factory of assistants, including one handsome boy with melting brown Umbrian eyes, something of a prodigy, whose father, Giovanni Santi, had been a minor painter in Perugia. The boy, Raphael (1483–1520), picked up Perugino's style quickly, and before long he was a first-rate Peruginesque painter.

Figure 13

But, having more than technical proficiency, Raphael was not content to remain a provincial. Before long he was to go to Florence, changing his style to accord with the more masculine and decisive taste of that city; later he would go on to Rome to enter the service of the pope and become something of a prince himself. We will have much more to say about him as one of the most successful and influential artists of the High Renaissance. But before he left Umbria when he was just past twenty he painted some small pictures in which the Umbrian spirit found its purest expression.

Raphael's *Vision of a Knight* (Plate C7) is filled with Peruginesque echoes, but it is not a formula picture. Its subject is appropriate for a talented and ambitious youth like Raphael. A boyish knight, whom it would be easy to identify with Raphael himself, lies asleep between two female figures. The one on the left holds a sword and a book, symbols of discipline and learning, which she offers the youth as a way of life. She is sensibly dressed, and her hair is held within a plain cap.

On the other side, a more alluring girl offers the less burdensome symbol of a bunch of flowers, perhaps primroses, the modest blossom that has become the symbol for a life of gaiety. This gentle temptress also wears a flower in her blond hair, and her charms are set off by floating veils, bead lacings, and draped flounces. To accentuate the irrevocable choice the knight must make before he begins his journey into the deep world behind him, the two candidates for his favor are sharply divided from one another by a sapling that cuts the picture in half. Before he died Raphael was to discover that these two ways of life need not be mutually exclusive, but his immediate choice was the sword, the book, and the sensible companion.

The Vision of a Knight is an uncomplicated picture whose poetic sweetness should be apparent. The idyllic landscape, the grace of the figures, the rich harmonies of reds, blues, and greens may be enjoyed at face value. It would

CLARVS INSIGNI VEHITVR TRIVMPHO ·
QVEM PAREM SVMMIS DVCIBVS PERHENNIS ·
FAMA VIRTVTVM CELEBRAT DECENTER ·
SCEPTRA TENENTEM ⌐

QVE MODVM REBVS TENVIT SECVNDIS ·
CONIVGIS MAGNI DECORATA RERVM ·
LAVDE GESTARVM VOLITAT PER ORA ·
CVNCTA VIRORVM ·

Alinari

Figure 14

be futile to try to extend their meaning, as we did with another picture of a young warrior, Andrea del Castagno's *Youthful David*.

Venice

Venice is a city so special that anything produced there takes on some of its individuality. Its art was influenced by the fantasy of a city whose buildings rise directly from the water, whose streets are canals, whose character of exotic richness originated during the centuries when it was the funnel between Europe and the Asia of spices and gold and jewels and silk. Venetian painting has always been marked by the double nature of magical vision and worldly opulence.

The opulence has worn a little thin today. The city is a little shabby, its commercially strategic position annihilated by new ways and routes of travel, its monuments left to tourists, and its palaces, lately, to café society. But not even the red and green traffic lights on the Grand Canal and the motor launches that

compete with gondolas can altogether tarnish this golden city. At worst it is a kind of celestial amusement park; at best it is still Venice.

The great century of Venetian painting will be treated in a later portfolio; now we must look at two early pictures, *The Miracle of the True Cross* (Plate C8) by Gentile Bellini, painted in 1500, and *The Dream of Saint Ursula* (*Figure 16*) by Vittore Carpaccio, signed and dated only five years before.

The Miracle of the True Cross tells the story of the rescue of a fragment of the True Cross, which, in its heavy reliquary, fell into a canal while it was being carried in a procession. In the foreground a white-robed monk, who has dived into the canal and touched the reliquary, is miraculously buoyed up and carried to the bank. Other figures, less fortunate, flounder in the water.

So far, the picture is straightforward enough, but the narrative is the least interesting and, for that matter, not the most conspicuous part. The setting has taken first place; this picture is really a portrait of a Venetian canal. Its bridge

Alinari

Figure 15

and houses and gondolas are painted with more loving attention than the chief actor in the miracle. The figures on the bridge are there for a special reason, but the effect is that of an ordinary city crowd in Venice. They are adjuncts to a cityscape. Rather disharmoniously, considering that we would expect them to be up and about their business, a group of gentlemen kneel reverently at the lower right, while their ladies stand in line on the bank at the left. Each head is the portrait of a Venetian dignitary or one of his womenfolk, and we are back again to Ghirlandaio's chatty descriptions of daily life.

An important difference, aside from the change of scene from a Florentine interior to a Venetian canal, is Bellini's treatment of light. Venetian painters were not only in love with their city as a mass of buildings; they were in love with Venice as a harmony of light, water, and air unique to its few wonderful square miles. Here the shimmer on the water, the glow in the sky, and the spread of illumination across the sides of the buildings mark the beginning of a preoccupation with the painting of light in air that will flower in the next century with Titian and Tintoretto and, continuing to affect European painting through the

22

centuries, culminate in the vibrant, prismatic light of impressionism.

Carpaccio's *Dream of Saint Ursula* also makes exceptional use of light, with the more specialized aim of creating magical ambiance. The picture is from a series telling Ursula's life; in this episode the young girl is told in a dream that she must follow a course of action that will end, as we are reminded by the symbolical palm branch carried by the angel, in her martyrdom.

What we have said about other pictures in which holy events take place in an ordinary interior must be forgotten here. Item by item the room is represented with as much precision as in Campin's *Annunciation* (Portfolio B, *Figure 19*) or in Ghirlandaio's palace interior. But the details are curiously isolated from one another, as if magically transfixed: the bedposts are strangely elongated; the plants in the windows exist, motionless, in patterns that seem only half real. Above all, the gentle light flowing through the door and reflected on objects in the room is an enchanted one in which ordinary things take on extraordinary qualities; it is like the light of early dawn, by which even the most familiar objects in our bedrooms take on a quiet, waiting, unfamiliar air.

Siena

And what, all this time, about Siena, that fortress of aristocratic medievalism in the century of science and exploration? We last referred to Sienese painters of the fourteenth century, in connection with Giotto, singling out the brothers Lorenzetti as exceptions among the Sienese, who, in general, rejected Giotto's innovations.

In the century of Masaccio and Piero della Francesca, Sienese painters continued to cultivate medievalism stubbornly, stylishly, and artificially, not because they were isolated by circumstance from the developments in Florence, which was only a few miles away, but because they took an almost snobbish pride in

Alinari

Figure 16

the conservative tradition of their own style. The reputation of only one Sienese painter, Francesco di Giorgio (1439–1502), extended significantly beyond his city. A sculptor, engineer, and architect, as well as a painter, he is credited by indirect evidence with the design of Federigo's perspective study in Gubbio, certainly not the work of a confirmed medievalist.

In the first half of the fifteenth century Siena's major painter was Sassetta (1392–1450); his *Saint Anthony Tempted by the Devil*

Figure 17

Figure 18

in the Form of a Woman (Portfolio 7, Plate 78) demonstrates his mastery of the compositional devices stemming from Duccio and his tactful continuation of the delicate precision of the Sienese version of the international style. It also, perhaps, hints at the anemia about to weaken and finally to starve a school of painting that deliberately isolated itself from contemporary life.

After Sassetta, Sienese forms became more and more attenuated and hypersensitive, like plants grown without sun. Giovanni di Paolo (about 1402–1482) was a prolific painter whose ingenious and decorative pictures always seem to be enacted on miniature stages by expensive dolls. His *Miracle of Saint Nicholas of Tolentino* (Plate C9) could hardly be more engaging, but it could hardly have less connection with the noble, dramatic power of the Renaissance, or with the true faith in miracle of the Middle Ages. Its charm lies in its conscious and skillful artificiality.

Upon a stormy sea, which Giovanni depicts as a field of uniform green hillocks, an ornamental ship is being torn apart by a tempest. Masts and sails fly into the air; they twist and flutter against a dark sky in patterns suggesting birds or serpents. The victims kneel in prayer on the spotless deck; above them Saint Nicholas appears as their savior. The most astonishing part of the picture is the naked sea goddess who swims gracefully beneath the water, trailing long golden locks, a curious pagan participant in this Christian anecdote. One need only compare Giovanni's *Expulsion of Adam and Eve from Paradise* (*Figure 17*) with Masaccio's painting to see the respective result of Sienese inbreeding and Florentine exploration. Obviously each picture has its special merits, but there can be no question as to which probes deeply into the nature of human experience and which offers us the kind of pleasure related to the cultivated niceties of fashion.

By the end of the century it was apparent that Sienese painting had exhausted its store of nourishment. At this late date the Sienese accepted the Renaissance and grafted the forms of certain second-rate renaissance artists onto their weakened style to produce, as the conclusion of a great tradition, some of the most unsatisfactory pictures in all painting.

Northern Italy

In northern Italy Andrea Mantegna (1431–1506) worked especially in the cities of Padua and Mantua but was the noblest Roman of them all. Mantegna would have been at home in the court of the Caesars; his work is a tribute to their triumphs, harsh vitality, strenuousness, and power. Much of Mantegna's most important work has disappeared. In the Second World War the history of destruction that has dogged him was tragically continued: his great frescoes in a chapel of the church of the Eremitani in Padua were lost when the apse was destroyed by bombing. The church is only a short walk from the Arena Chapel; only the negative consolation that Giotto's frescoes were spared can reconcile us to the loss of so magnificent a cycle. At present the remaining fragments are being patched together as well as is possible.

The Eremitani frescoes represented scenes from the lives and martyrdoms of early Christian saints. *Saint James Led to Martyr-*

Figure 19

25

Figure 20

26

dom (*Figure 18*) gives an idea of the bitter force of Mantegna's style. The Eremitani panels were painted as though the wall were divided into a series of stages or compartments, one above the other, opening into deep perspectives. *Saint James Led to Martyrdom*, like others on the upper levels, was painted in illusionistic perspective. The observer seems to look at a scene being enacted above him, but every detail, even those far back in space, is represented with the sharp clarity of close vision.

Of all the painters in this century who were infatuated with classical antiquity, Mantegna came closest to archaeological accuracy. We shall see in the next portfolio paintings by Botticelli and other artists for whom classicism was a reverie, a dream, or an exercise in the intellectual manipulation of legend. But we cannot look at Mantegna's pictures without feeling that for him antiquity was real, that the fragments of Roman architecture and sculpture in his studio evoked a Rome free from the mists of recollection or the hazards of supposition. His Rome is so real, so factual, so strong, so vivid, so overpoweringly convincing, that we accept it as true, even though scholarship since the time of Mantegna may have modified his concept of Rome. No matter; here is an arrogant, military Rome of a masculinity that would be brutal if it were not so precisely studied, of a stoicism that would be bitter if it were not, at the same time, so rich.

Mantegna's *Martyrdom of Saint Sebastian* (Plate C10) demonstrates that for this Christian painter Christian stories were most interesting when they were closely tied to the Roman scene. His Sebastian is a hard-fleshed Roman youth who suffers torture without flinching; the Roman fragments (*Figure 19*) are as interesting to Mantegna as the musculature of the body, which, as much as any Florentine, he studied scientifically. Mantegna knew the Florentines who visited Padua and Mantua—Uccello, Fra Filippo Lippi, Donatello, and Alberti, whose church in Mantua

was designed after a Roman triumphal arch. In his science and his classicism, Mantegna equalled if not outstripped them.

As a colorist Mantegna ranged from the all-but-frigid tonality of *Saint Sebastian*, appropriate to the severity of the conception, to Venetian brilliance (he was a brother-in-law of Gentile Bellini and his brother Giovanni). His small panels, especially, are intense in color; *The Adoration of the Shepherds* (Portfolio 7, Plate 82), for instance, is set in a world of fantastically hued rocks, blasted trees, sudden eruptions of rich foliage, infinite distances, and crystalline air in which colors gleam with supernatural brilliance. Mantegna's forms seem carved as much as painted—carved from cold stone, sometimes from bright jewels. The wrinkles in the face of Sebastian's executioner (*Figure 20*) could have been chiseled in granite.

Leonardo da Vinci

So much has been written about Leonardo da Vinci (1452–1519) that one feels reluctant to add to it. The facts of his life are apparently as well known as they are ever to be; its mysteries have been the subject of endless speculation; its legends have become hopelessly ingrained with both. But no discussion of the art of the fifteenth century in Italy can conclude without some summary of Leonardo as an artist who gathered together the achievements of his century and yet defeated its intention.

Leonardo's paintings represent only a small fraction of his contribution to the world and an even smaller fraction of his potential contribution. We say "potential" because his notebooks are filled with diagrams for inventions (telescopes, printing presses, gears, even an armored tank) that he never bothered to build. As a public man Leonardo was a painter, a sculptor, a musician, an engineer, an inventor, and a mathematical theorist, but in his private world he pondered nothing less than the total question of man's being.

For the other contemporary artist-scientists, notably Piero della Francesca, learning was directed toward a crystallization of man's relationship to his world in specific terms that assumed the possibility of a neat and harmonious conclusion of the problem. The precise geometrical scheme of Leonardo's *Last Supper* (Portfolio 6, Plate 61) is in line with this concept, by which mathematical order became the renaissance artist's means to express man's imposition of order and security on the world. But Leonardo studied the movement of clouds, the erosion of rocks, the flow of water, the nature of minerals, the root systems of plants, the internal organs of the body. He observed the facts of nature less as practical science than as metaphysics and especially ontology, the science of being. Leonardo's concern was cosmology, the fundamental causes and process in things, the whole problem of creation, existence, and life, which still occupies philosophers and scientists and remains unexplained.

All the parts of the universal scheme, which somehow must hold the secret of being, were collected, categorized, and pigeonholed in the Middle Ages against a background of unquestioned belief in divine creation. Leonardo could not accept this conviction as a fact. His *Virgin of the Rocks* (Plate C11) is set in a grotto resembling an astral landscape or a primeval world where rocks, water, and plants suggest the beginnings of things, the sources of life. Placing the Virgin and child, images of man's redemption, against this background puts man at the center of an inexplicable universe, one that, as Leonardo presents it, remains a mystery though its elements are specifically detailed.

All the hundreds of interpretations offered for *The Virgin of the Rocks* accept its air of mystery. Any explanation must begin by relating the concept of God to the concept of a world created by natural forces. The Virgin and child are not presented as Fra Angelico, for instance, would present them—with un-questioning acceptance of their reality; rather, they symbolize man's need for a faith to reassure him in a world that he cannot explain, to give point to an otherwise bewildering existence.

Leonardo, who was born just at the middle of the fifteenth century, lived nineteen years into the next one. The triumvirate of painters for this magnificent period is, then: at its beginning, Masaccio, who gave it direction and impetus; at midpoint, Piero, who completed the synthesis of art and science; and, at its end, Leonardo. Leonardo's scientific knowledge exceeded that of any other man of his time, but his art turned inward in such a way that even a serene picture like *The Virgin of the Rocks* contains the germ of first doubt, questioning the assumption that objective investigation could infallibly reveal man's inner nature.

The direction and all the exploration of renaissance thought had been based on the premise that the world was a rational place whose secrets need only to be ferreted out systematically to uncover its inner order. But Leonardo, who ferreted the secrets out as no one else had done before, leaves us with the realization that they lead eventually not to clarification but to mystery and that knowledge leads ultimately to enigma.

Leonardo never stated this conclusion, unless he implied it in the smile of the *Mona Lisa* (Portfolio 1, Plate 6). But it became inevitable when science explored far enough to show that a world that had been thought finite was just the reverse—infinite and complicated beyond total explanation. And the conclusion was terrifying in its suggestion that science was a false mistress who, having lured man from faith, now failed him, leaving him bereft, without anchor or compass in an infinite and troubled sea.

It is necessary to repeat that this conclusion was not reached by Leonardo; it is only implied by the curiously disturbing sum of his life and work. For that matter, it was never quite accepted in Italy—or at least it never

29

Figure 21

troubled the Italians very much. Its melancholy premise took root in the north, where Shakespeare, a hundred years later, personified it in the character of Hamlet. But another northerner, Albrecht Dürer (1471–1528), stated it much earlier in his *Melancholia I* (Portfolio 10, *Figure 9*), which was engraved in 1514.

Dürer

The woman in *Melancholia I*, surrounded by symbols of science and learning, seems to brood on their impotence. The allegory takes on special pertinence if we compare it with Federigo's perspective study (*Figure 12*), where the same symbols are used. In Dürer's engraving the objects are heaped around in confusion, but in the good duke's study they are disposed in intimate and reassuring order. In the study, learning and science surround one protectively; in the engraving, they are the paraphernalia of frustration.

Melancholia I and the Isenheim altarpiece (Plate B11 and *Figure 23*), which closed our discussion of medieval painting, were completed within a year or so of one another, bringing us neatly to a mutual concluding point. But Dürer, unlike his contemporary Grünewald, was a renaissance man. For us he is the first representative of the interchange between the two sides of the Alps that, almost overnight, was to bring the Renaissance to the north. An early visit to Italy brought him into contact with renaissance artists—the influence of Mantegna is apparent in his work. More importantly, he brought back the renaissance idea of the artist as an individual who might be courted by princes, an intellectual among intellectuals rather than a craftsman. His *Self-Portrait* (Plate C12) shows a man keenly and proudly aware of his individuality, yet without conceit or arrogance. On a second trip to Italy his reputation had preceded him, and he was feted everywhere.

To avoid giving the impression that Dürer's art was one of pessimism and defeat, *Melancholia I* must be paired with a usual companion piece of the same date, *Saint Jerome in His Study* (*Figure 21*), in which the artist shows the joys of studious contemplation, the satisfactions of learning, and the faith in intellect that formed the core of the early Renaissance and brought into being the pictures discussed in this portfolio. Jerome's study is flooded with happy light in which the saint's symbol, the lion, basks as contentedly as a house cat. In these two engravings Dürer recognizes the varying nature and experience of man, who, having chosen himself as the master of his fate, is responsible for the direction of his life.

Color Plates

Figures
in the Text